ETHEREUM

— — — — — ❦❧ — — — — —

Your Guide To Understanding Ethereum,
Blockchains, and Cryptocurrency

Tim Mathis

liable for any hardship or damages that may befall them after undertaking information described herein.

Additionally, the information in the following pages is intended only for informational purposes and should thus be thought of as universal. As befitting its nature, it is presented without assurance regarding its prolonged validity or interim quality. Trademarks that are mentioned are done without written consent and can in no way be considered an endorsement from the trademark holder.

Table of Contents

Introduction

Although we commonly associate the blockchain technology and cryptocurrency with Bitcoin, there is far more to it than that.

Blockchain technology has a lot of other practical uses right now, with much more in the pipeline, all of which go beyond the digital currency. Nowadays, Bitcoin is just one of hundreds of applications using the technology.

Until recently, to build a blockchain application, you would have needed a very complex background in cryptography, coding, and math and you would have needed a lot of resources too. Things have changed and now using the blockchain is far easier than anyone could have imagined, with uses ranging from electronic voting, property, and asset recording to compliance and trading. One of the tools that makes all this possible is Ethereum.

We all call Bitcoin the king of the cryptocurrency world and that makes Ethereum the queen. In this book, we will be discussing what the blockchain is before we move on to Ethereum as well as what it's all about and what you can do with it. For now, suffice to say that the price of Ethereum is fast rising and it is now becoming one of the most promising of all the cryptocurrencies. Want to learn more? Read on and I will tell you all you need to know.

A Guide to the Blockchain

W hat is this blockchain we keep hearing so much about? Before I go into too many details, let's look at a brief example:

Imagine a Google spreadsheet, one that every computer in the world shares and a spreadsheet that is connected to the internet. Each time something happens, a transaction for example, it will be recorded on a separate row on the spreadsheet.

Anyone who has a computer or a mobile device can log onto the internet and can see the spreadsheet. They can see every transaction that happens on the spreadsheet and they can add another transaction if they want. The only thing they cannot do is make any changes to the transactions that are already on there.

That is, in essence, the blockchain. Nice and easy, isn't it? Where the spreadsheet has rows, a blockchain has blocks. Each block is a collection of data and each bit of data is added by the connection of one block to the last and so on in chronological order. These connected blocks make a chain.

Therefore, the blockchain is a global database, online, that anyone who has an internet connection can view and use. Because this database exists on the net, it is classed as decentralized – the ledger or database is shared between every computer in the world, not just stored in one specific location with limited access.

This is what makes cryptocurrencies like Bitcoin and Ethereum so unique.

Bitcoin and the Blockchain

The first application for the blockchain, and perhaps the most famous, is Bitcoin, a P2P digital currency. A Bitcoin is created through mining and is stored on the blockchain. Unlike the physical money we use today, Bitcoin can be sent to anyone and to anywhere without the need to go through a bank or a government or any other agency that might want to interfere and take their cut from you.

The blockchain really doesn't care whether you are a machine, a human, or even a dog. The security in the blockchain comes from the verification of each transaction by all the nodes, or computers, that are on the blockchain network and that eliminates the need for all those expensive intermediaries.

How does the blockchain work and why can't anyone hack into it?

We know what the blockchain is now, so let's look at how they work. I will stick with using Bitcoin for this because it is one of the easiest and better-known examples.

In the Bitcoin blockchain, there is a series of 1 MB blocks, each of which contains P2P transactions. A block is added to the chain every 10 minutes, following verification by the Bitcoin miner network and a consensus mechanism that is built into the system. Each of the entries within a block is fully secured using cryptographic math, making the transaction irreversible. The blocks in the chain have the following features:

- Each one is time-stamped with the date and time

- Each one is decentralized and distributed – there are multiple copies of each block stored in multiple locations

- Each one is transparent, which means anyone can see what is on it

Irreversible

When a transaction takes place on the Bitcoin blockchain, it is sent to a pool that contains transactions not yet verified. These transactions will then be grouped together in one block, every 10 minutes, and Bitcoin miners will then work at solving a computational math problem, which is very difficult. When the problem is solved, the transactions are verified and the block is added to the chain.

Because blocks are added regularly, it gets more difficult to reverse any transaction or to double-spend the Bitcoin used in a transaction. At the same time, the Bitcoin blockchain is used by many millions of users, each of whom runs the ledger on their own computers – akin to having millions of copies of the Bitcoin ledger, right from the very first block ever mined.

These copies all contain the history of every block since Bitcoin started and this is what makes it so difficult to hack. If that weren't enough, each of the transactions is fully secured with cryptographic math. If anyone were to attempt to change the ledger they would need to be able to hack into 51% of the network – that means having to hack 51% of the total computers on the network running that ledger at the same time. This would require an amount of capital that is eye watering, not to mention the electric energy required and this is what makes it unlikely that anyone will ever hack the blockchain or attempt to tamper with it. Not only that, but in a situation like this, the value of the Bitcoin would significantly plummet, making it worthless to hold them.

Bitcoin is just one example of a blockchain, but the blockchain can be implemented across any number of industries and used to solve various problems.

Why Does the Blockchain Matter?

The blockchain matters because it is a transparent and immutable records database and this is what ensures that no third-party needs to get involved. Think about it with this example:

> A farmer in Africa owns a nice piece of land but he has lost his copy of the agreement and the deed in a flood. Because of that, he can't prove he owned that land. There was a digital copy of that agreement, but that was stored on a government database and that too was destroyed. What does he do? Had that deed and agreement been filed on a blockchain, he would have had no trouble verifying that he was the true owner of the land.

This is just one example of how the blockchain is useful. As well as verifying ownership, it will also help to protect your identity, avoid the situation of double-spending, and may, in the future, even run autonomous vehicles.

The Future of the Blockchain

It really is no exaggeration when I say that the blockchain will, in the future, be an integral and important feature in our lives. The success or otherwise of cryptocurrencies like Bitcoin will have no bearing on the future of the blockchain because the blockchain is way bigger than any cryptocurrency, even Bitcoin. Some of the more notable moves in the blockchain ecosystem are:

- In 2016, the technology attracted an investment of $1.4 billion.

- In 2016, the government in Dubai announced that, by 2020, all their supply chain will be on the blockchain.

- Ethereum has recently established the Ethereum Enterprise Alliance – EEA, while IBM is working on a new blockchain technology called Hyperledger.

- Over 50 of the biggest financial companies in the world are running experiments with the blockchain.

When it's all said and done, the only thing that will tell us just how disruptive this innovative technology is going to be is time.

A Guide to Ethereum

In the most basic form, Ethereum is a blockchain-based open-source platform that gives developers the opportunity to build decentralized applications and deploy them. Like Bitcoin, it is a distributed blockchain network that is public, but there are some significant differences between the two.

The most significant difference is in the purpose and the capability of the two networks. Bitcoin offers a specific blockchain application, that of a P2P digital cash system that allows for online payments of Bitcoin. This network is used for tracking the ownership of the Bitcoin, but Ethereum is focused on the program code needed to run a decentralized application.

With the Ethereum blockchain, the miners will work to earn Ether or ETH rather than Bitcoin. Although this is a type of digital currency, rather than being spent in the same way we make purchases with Bitcoin, ETH is the fuel that is needed to run the Ethereum network. It can be traded, but is generally used by the application developers to pay for the services and the transaction fees on the Ethereum network.

Smart Contracts

In a later chapter, I will show you how to build a smart contract, but for now, we are just going to look at what they are and what they can be used for. A smart contract is a piece of computer code that contains instructions for a transaction or exchange of something of value to take place when certain conditions are met. Because they are programmed to run on the blockchain, these contract act exactly as they should and execute exactly when they are programmed to do so without the interference of any third-party and without the risk of hacking or downtime.

All blockchains can process code, but most of them are limited in what they can do. That is where Ethereum differs; instead of developers being curtailed by a limit on operations, they can create the operations they want to use. This means there is the potential for thousands of applications that can go beyond anything ever seen before.

The Virtual Machine

Before Ethereum came into existence, blockchain applications could only be designed to do limited things. The cryptocurrencies were designed to do one thing – operate as P2P digital currencies, nothing more. This posed a problem for developers – they either had to expand the range of functions that these cryptocurrencies could do, which would be complicated and take too much time, or they could come up with a new kind of blockchain-based platform and application. The developer of Ethereum, Vitalik Buterin, therefore, came up with an innovative approach.

The core innovation of Ethereum is the EVM, or Ethereum Virtual Machine. It is a Turing-complete software running on the Ethereum network, enabling anybody to run whatever program they want regardless of what programming language it is written in, given sufficient memory and time. The EVM simplifies the process of creating blockchain-based applications and makes it all more efficient. Rather than needing to build a new blockchain for each application, the EVM enables thousands of different apps to be built on one single platform.

What Can We Use Ethereum for?

Ethereum is primarily for developers to build their decentralized applications on and to deploy them from. Otherwise known as Dapps, these applications will serve a specific purpose. Bitcoin is a Dapp that provides the P2P digital cash system for example. Because these applications are comprised of code that runs on the blockchain, no one person or entity controls them.

Think of all the different intermediary services that are used across different industries. From banks to other services that we rarely give a second thought to, like regulatory compliance, voting systems, etc., if the service is centralized, it can easily be decentralized with Ethereum.

We can also use Ethereum to build DAOs – Decentralized Autonomous Organizations. These are decentralized organizations that are fully autonomous, having no one leader. They are run purely by programming code, smart contracts that have been written on Ethereum. This code replaces the structure and the rules of a traditional organization and eliminates the need for centralized control and for people. Each DAO is owned by those who purchase ETH tokens but, rather than the tokens acting as equity shares or ownership, they provide the token owner with voting rights instead.

The Benefits of Ethereum

Because all these decentralized applications will run on the blockchain, they will all benefit from the properties of the blockchain:

- **Immutable** – *changes cannot be made to any data by a third party.*

- **Tamper-proof and corruption-free** – *the framework the apps are built on are based on the principle of consensus and this makes censorship virtually impossible.*

- **Secure** – *there is no single point of failure and all applications and transactions are secured with cryptography, giving them strong protection against fraud and hacking.*

- **No downtime** – *the blockchain can't go down so the apps can't go down and they are never switched off.*

The Downside to Decentralized Applications

Although the decentralized application comes with many benefits, it is not completely without fault. The code for the smart contracts are written by humans and they are only as good as whoever writes them. Any oversights, bugs in the code, or sheer human error can lead to things happening that weren't meant to and if a mistake is exploited, there is absolutely no efficient way to stop it – the only way would be to get consensus from the network and rewrite the underlying code. This is not what the blockchain is all about because it is meant to be immutable and any action that a central party does will raise questions about the apparent decentralized nature of the application.

How Do I Access Ethereum to Develop an App?

There are lots of ways to plug yourself into the Ethereum network, but by far the best and easiest is to use the native Mist browser. Mist is user-friendly and provides you with a digital wallet for storage and trade of ETH tokens – later I will show you how to set up a Mist wallet. Mist also allows you to write smart contracts and manage them, deploying them and using them. Like a normal web browser provides access to the net and helps you to navigate it, so Mist is a portal to the decentralized blockchain application world.

You can also use a browser extension called MetaMask. This transforms Google Chrome to an Ethereum browser and lets anyone develop or run a decentralized app from the browser.

Although it was first built as a plugin for Chrome, in time it will also provide support for Firefox and other platforms.

They are in their early days yet, but Mist and MetaMask, not to mention other browsers, are starting to give us more access to decentralized applications. Even if you are not from a technical background, you can still build that decentralized application, a revolutionary jump that could bring the Dapp firmly into the mainstream.

What Dapps Are Being Developed Now?

Ethereum is currently being used as a platform for applications covering a wide range of industries and different services. However, this is uncharted territory for developers, so at this stage, it is difficult to know what will and won't be a success. Some of the more exciting projects are:

- **Weifund** – an open-source platform aimed at crowdfunding for smart contracts. The platform helps contributions to be turned into digital assets, backed up by a contract that can be traded, used, or sold on the Ethereum platform.

- **Uport** – gives users a convenient and secure method of taking control of their personal information and identity. Rather than having to rely on government agencies and giving up their identities to intermediaries, users have full control over who can see ad use their information and data.

- **BlockApps** - is trying to provide enterprises with an easier way to build blockchain apps and manage them. All the tools needed are provided, from proof of concept to legacy system integration and full production for blockchain applications that are industry-specific, private or public.

- **Provenance** – makes use of Ethereum to make supply chains somewhat more transparent. They allow for the tracing of a product's origin and a full history of it, giving customers a more open and easily accessible information framework to base their purchasing decisions on.

- **Augur** – a market platform for prediction and forecasting, it allows people to forecast events and rewards them for correct predictions. Any predictions made on real-world events are done through the trade of virtual shares and if shares are bought by a person who wins a prediction they are given a monetary reward.

The DAO Hack

We know that Ethereum is a platform for building Decentralized Autonomous apps, but in 2016 something went very wrong. A startup group who was working on a project called The DAO were hacked. This project was being developed by a team called lock.it with the aim of producing a venture capital firm that would not require human employees. People would be able to use smart contracts to make their decisions. The DAO received funding through the sale of ETH tokens and raised around $150 million from thousands of sources.

An unknown attacker struck shortly after that money was raised and stole around $50 million of ETH. This attack came about through a single flaw in the DAO software, NOT the Ethereum platform, but it left the founders and the developers of Ethereum having to clean up the mess.

Much debate took place and the entire Ethereum community held a vote. The outcome was to retrieve the funds through a Hard Fork, or by changing the code. The fork moved the stolen money into a new smart contract, one that allowed the original owners to get their ETH tokens. Things got a bit complicated at this point with the implications proving somewhat controversial. Here's why that happened.

Ethereum is based on the blockchain technology that is not meant to be reversible; transactions are not supposed to be able to be changed. The decision to execute the hard fork, effectively disregarding all the rules that dictate how a blockchain executes, resulted in a very dangerous precedent being set, one that goes against the reason for the blockchain. If the blockchain were to change whenever a large amount of ETH was involved or whenever a large group of investors was impacted negatively, the blockchain is going to lose the value proposition that backs it up - the value of being secure, unchangeable, tamper-proof, and anonymous.

A slightly less aggressive solution was put forward but the Ethereum founders and the community as a whole were put in a dodgy situation. If the stolen funds weren't retrieved, confidence in the platform would plummet. On the other hand, to recover the money would require actions that went against the value propositions of the platform and would set an incredibly dangerous precedent.

A majority vote went in favor of the hard fork, but as not everyone agreed, the result was a split with two blockchains running parallel to one another. Ethereum Classic is for those investors who do not agree with changes being made to the blockchain, even in the case of hacking, while Ethereum remains for those who agreed to rewrite a bit of the code and retrieve the stolen funds.

The Future of Ethereum

Despite all this, Ethereum continues to move forward and the future is looking very bright. The platform is user-friendly and it gives people the opportunity to use the power of the blockchain, thus speeding up decentralization across the world economy. These decentralized applications have enormous potential in causing huge disruption to hundreds of different industries. Most of the more significant organizations will use private blockchains to run their business processes.

- **Private Blockchain** – inside the next couple of years, some of the major companies will be using private, permissioned blockchains to run some of their business processes, giving employees, service providers, vendors, and customers alike access to the business blockchain through transactions that are cryptographically authenticated.

- **Consortia Blockchain** – consortia blockchains will be on the rise within the next couple of years, providing collaboration for counterparties on use cases that will allow the sharing of trusted source-of-truth value, supply, and infrastructure chains.

- **Public Blockchain – Business Use** – some companies are expected to use the public Ethereum platform for use cases with the same blockchain components that they use on their private blockchain implementations.

The Ethereum platform is also starting to change the way we use the internet. Dapps are pushing for a change from the Internet of Information we are all used to using for viewing and exchanging information, over to an Internet of Value, where immediate value can be exchanged without the need for intermediaries. It is in its early days yet and there is a lot of work to be done, but there is no doubt that Ethereum is going to be one of the most revolutionary platforms and that exciting times await us.

The Ethereum Blockchain

Today, Bitcoin continues to be the largest, open public blockchain and serves as the definitive model upon which many other blockchain-based applications are based. However, the Bitcoin blockchain is only one implementation of blockchain technology. As more and more industries begin to explore the potential of blockchain, new models are emerging on a regular basis, often designed to serve a specific purpose.

When we look at Bitcoin, we see that fundamentally its purpose is a decentralized, peer-to-peer digital currency. Bitcoin solves a particular problem: how to make secure financial transactions on a peer-to-peer basis from anywhere in the world while eliminating the need for trust, a middleman, or centralized authority like a bank. While Bitcoin is not perfect, it has been quite successful in terms of serving the purpose for which it was intended.

As developers and entrepreneurs began to see implications for blockchain technology that went far beyond financial transactions, many began to imagine alternative blockchain structures that might be more suited to different functions. Vitalik Buterin, the developer of Ethereum, envisioned an open platform upon which anybody could build a blockchain-based application to perform any kind of function.

ETHEREUM

Rather than a blockchain that simply stored financial transaction data, as with Bitcoin, the Ethereum blockchain is designed to execute code based on verified transactions. Instead of simply moving funds from Account A to Account B, as with Bitcoin, Ethereum could create an environment where a transaction from Account A to Account B could trigger a vast range of events. For example, transactions in Ethereum can be used to register a new domain name, transfer property titles, manage voter registration, or execute secure contracts between two or more parties. In fact, "transactions" within Ethereum are often referred to as "smart contracts."

Smart Contracts in Ethereum

T he term "smart contract" comes up a lot in reference to Ethereum. What is a smart contract? The short answer is that a smart contract is a computer program. Smart contracts are really the "meat and potatoes" of Ethereum, and it is worth exploring this concept in some depth in order to really grasp the power and vision of the platform.

If you don't have much in the way of technical background, don't worry. When it comes to actually **writing** smart contracts you will need to learn to code or hire a programmer, but you don't need to know how to code in order to understand, conceptually, how smart contracts work. However, it is helpful to have a basic understanding of how computer programs work, even if you don't necessarily know how to write them yourself.

While they can do incredibly complex things, all computer programs essentially work by asking a series of yes or no questions. When we think about all "data" ultimately consisting of 1's and 0's, or binary code, what those 1's and 0's represent are "yes's" and "no's". Broadly speaking, there are no "maybes" for a computer. If we could write a simple computer program in English, it might look something like this:

> Dear computer, if I am playing a video and I click the pause button, then please pause the video.

In this example, the computer will first need to check if I am playing a video. This is the first "yes or no" question it will need to answer. If the answer is "yes," I am playing a video, then it will ask question number two: am I clicking the pause button? Let's say I'm not. For as long as I am playing the video (i.e. as long as the first answer is still "yes"), the computer will wait, patiently, asking that second question over and over again until the answer is "yes." It's only mission in life, as long as I am playing a video, is to check constantly whether or not I am pressing the pause button. As soon as I do press the pause button, the answer to the second question becomes "yes," and then it will pause the video.

When we think about digital transactions happening with Bitcoin, what we're really doing when we participate in these transactions is executing a simple computer program. The essence of what happens is that Person A sends funds to Person B. Bitcoin's software will ask a series of questions: Does Person A actually have sufficient funding? Can Person A verify ownership of the address holding those funds? Is the address for Person B valid? As long as the correct inputs are provided, the decentralized Bitcoin network will reach a consensus for performing the computations and executing the program: the transaction will be verified and Person B will receive the funds.

With Bitcoin, the program that is running **only deals with one type of transaction**. "Bitcoins" are essentially just numbers that are moved around from one digital address to another, and the record of all of those moves is stored on the blockchain. The blockchain provides a system for a decentralized network of computers to reach a consensus about which tasks to perform and then to perform said tasks.

In the case of Bitcoin, the "tasks" are transfers of coin from Person A to Person B, but is there any reason why this system couldn't be used to handle other types of tasks? Well, no, and that is precisely what Ethereum is built to do. Ethereum uses the same blockchain infrastructure, but it opens the door for **any type of program** to be executed.

Even when we continue to think in terms of financial transactions, the possibilities that Ethereum offers allow for things like conditions, creating a much more flexible environment for payment systems. For example, with Ethereum, a secure deposit could be held on the blockchain for a specified period of time: if a set of conditions were not met, it could be returned to the payer; if the conditions were met, the payment could be released to the receiver. In Bitcoin, there is no way to hold a payment in "escrow" like this without the use of a third party. This kind of conditional transaction is a simple example of something that could be executed with a smart contract in Ethereum.

Another use for smart contracts can include a 'multi-signature' approach to releases funds, meaning that a specified number of people must all agree to release the funds in order for the contract to be fulfilled. To further complicate matters, but also to make them much more exciting, smart contracts are actually often used to trigger **other** smart contracts. For example, let's say you wanted to place a bet that your favorite sports team was going to win their next game: You could use one contract to place the bet, and in the background another smart contract would be used to gather data about the game and process the results, which would then send the outcome back to yet another smart contract to handle dispensing payout to the winner.

As we become more integrated into the Internet of Things, smart contracts open up a whole world of possibilities. For example, as smart cars become more prevalent, we could easily envision a transition from the old system of needing to put money in a parking meter to a system that would run entirely on smart contracts. Sensors could easily link specific cars to specific parking spaces, and a smart contract could be used to automatically deduct the appropriate fee based on the time a car was parked in a given space. Rather than digging around for change under the seat and dealing with parking meters, drivers could just park and the smart contract would manage the transaction in the background. Cities could do away with the system of meter maids and automate the entire process.

The concept of a supply chain can also serve as a good example for visualizing how smart contracts can be linked together in a real-world scenario. Let's say you go to a store and buy a toothbrush. This store normally only has 10 of these toothbrushes in stock, and you buy the last one. Many more are housed at a warehouse 100 miles away. They are manufactured, however, in China. The chemical plant that supplies the plastic to make this toothbrush is actually located in Texas.

At the point of exchange, when you buy the toothbrush, a network of smart contracts could immediately inform the warehouse that the store needs more inventory, which would in turn inform the manufacturer that they will need to get another shipment ready for the warehouse, which will in turn let the plastic supplier know that, in order to make more toothbrushes, the factory in China will need to have more raw materials shipped over to them.

The advantages to automating this entire system via smart contracts include eliminating a huge amount of paperwork, bureaucracy, delays, human error, and fees associated with middlemen required in each instance to physically contact the next link up in the supply chain and negotiate each order. Making these incredibly complex systems more efficient and less vulnerable to corruption by creating a transparent record of every transaction is one of the most promising applications for smart contracts.

Despite the fundamental differences between Bitcoin and Ethereum, many people tend to treat these two projects as "competitors," battling for control of the blockchain space. Even for those who are only interested in Ether as a currency, and don't care particularly about the technology, this mindset is not really accurate. Ultimately, Bitcoin and Ethereum are two distinct, coexisting technologies that have different goals and applications. Bitcoin is designed to be a currency: it is an end in and of itself. Ethereum utilizes Ether as a way to execute smart contracts: the Ether currency is a means to end. In this sense, the two projects are not really competitors, in that they both have different visions, goals, and uses.

In order to further grasp the concept of smart contracts and how the Ethereum platform works, it is useful to explore some of the fundamentals of software development. If you have some experience working with any programming language, you will have an advantage in terms of understanding the way code is executed using smart contracts. If not, don't worry. Again, you don't actually need to know how to write code in order to understand how Ethereum works, but it is useful to become familiar with some basic programming concepts.

Understanding the Concept of "State" in Applications

Within software development, there is a concept known as "state." Very basically, state refers to what is happening within an application at any given moment in time. Whenever something changes, that application's state changes.

For example, imagine you are visiting a web page that requires you to sign up for an account. You would most likely need to fill in a form with some information and click a "Submit" button to send your form to the website's server. You would then be taken to a "Welcome" page and given access to the rest of the website. Behind the scenes, when you send in the form and the website takes you to the Welcome page, the **state** of the program being executed on the website changes.

Why does this matter? Smart contracts in Ethereum are ultimately programs or applications. Each iteration of an application's state is stored on the blockchain. This might sound complicated - and it is, in fact, pretty complicated - but this record of a program's history is fundamental to how smart contracts work in Ethereum. Within Ethereum applications, when a "transaction" occurs, software code can be triggered and executed. Thus, the state of that application can be changed and a record of what happened within the code is stored on the blockchain. By maintaining this record, the entire history of any given application's execution can be accessed and used to verify claims and regulate transactions.

The Ethereum Virtual Machine (EVM)

A ll of the machines participating in the Ethereum network are called "nodes." Much like Bitcoin and other decentralized peer-to-peer networks, there are many nodes spread out all across the world. Anybody can choose to run a node. In terms of Ethereum, we can think of all of these different computers merging together, in a sense, to form one giant computer capable of performing distributed computations. This concept is known as the "Ethereum Virtual Machine," often abbreviated to EVM.

Virtual machines (or VM's), in computing terms, are emulated computer systems. If you've ever partitioned your hard-drive to run both Windows and OSX, you've used one kind of virtual machine. For our purposes, we don't really need to know too much about the role of virtual machines, in general. When it comes to the Ethereum Virtual Machine, the thing that is important to know is that it is the **runtime environment** for smart contracts. Each node on the Ethereum network runs an implementation of the EVM.

Like most virtual machines, the Ethereum Virtual Machine works at a very low-level, meaning that it processes code written in a "low-level" programming language. For developers, writing smart contracts is a lot more efficient when done in a "high-level" language. So, smart contracts are written in one language, usually Solidity, and then compiled (using a special program called a "compiler") into the low-level code that can be processed by the EVM environment.

Smart contracts run on the Ethereum Virtual Machine, which runs on each participating node. When we consider what we know about blockchain technology and what we have just covered concerning Ethereum, a few questions may arise.

First, if every instance of an application's state is stored on the blockchain, doesn't that mean the blockchain will become really, really big? Won't that make it difficult for nodes to continuously maintain it? How can smaller nodes use the network efficiently if they don't have the capacity to store the entire state? Good question!

If the Ethereum blockchain used the same approach and structure as Bitcoin- that is, if it simply recorded a long list of every single thing ever that happened with every application- it would indeed create problems in terms of efficiency and scalability. As you may have guessed, this is not exactly how it works.

In fact, this is one of the facets of the Ethereum blockchain that makes it unique, diverging from the architecture of the original blockchain as implemented by Bitcoin. Ethereum uses a particular kind of data structure based on a mathematical principle called a Merkle Tree. Bitcoin's blockchain also uses a Merkle Tree, but to get technical, Ethereum actually uses a special kind of Merkle Tree known as a Merkle Patricia Tree.

The Merkle Patricia Tree used by Ethereum is a way of storing data (i.e. the data that makes up the "blocks") as a set of key/value pairs. A "key" is a short code that corresponds to a specific "value," which can be a much longer piece of data.

These keys and values are generated and authenticated using cryptographically secure algorithms. Keys and values can only be generated in one very specific way using a particular mathematical method that only works in one-direction. What this means is that any data (the value) that is fed into the algorithm will result in the same key every time. However, you cannot reverse the process by feeding a key into the system to arrive at the initial value.

Given the same set of keys and values, you would get the exact same Merkle Tree structure each and every time. Even a slight change in one bit of input data will yield a completely different output. Conceptually, this is the most important detail to grasp in terms of how verification works: **any data that you feed into the algorithm will generate the identical cryptographically secure output each time as long as the data remains unchanged.**

Thus far, what we have described is pretty much the same as the Merkle Trees that are used in the Bitcoin blockchain. What makes Ethereum's model different is the "Patricia" part of the Merkle Patricia Tree. This has to do with how the keys are positioned throughout the blockchain's data structure.

Getting into the mathematical logic behind the scenes is a bit beyond the scope of this book, but broadly speaking, the system is able to decide how to merge and arrange data stored in blocks by using prefixes that are assigned to each key. What this means, practically speaking, is that nodes have the ability to verify authenticity without needing to download the entire blockchain.

In fact, individual nodes will almost never need to access the entire state of the system to perform a given computation. Downloading the entire blockchain, therefore, would not be very efficient. Instead, a node can download only the partial state that it needs, and it can verify that chunk of code (or that "branch of the tree") by checking it against the surrounding branches using the keys. Because the surrounding branches will contain a reference linked all the way back to the root (the very first transaction), nodes can verify the partial state without needing to download the entire state history. This makes transactions in Ethereum much faster, more efficient, and allows for greater scalability of the platform.

The Role of Ether in Smart Contracts

Smart contracts, we have learned, are computer programs, or "scripts," written in code. These scripts are written in a Turing-complete programming language. "Turing-complete," by definition, means that this language is capable of doing any kind of computation. If something can be expressed with an algorithm, a Turing-complete language can express it. While there are a few languages that can be used to write smart contracts, the most popular today is called Solidity. Solidity is similar in many ways to JavaScript, a very versatile and widely used programming language notable for its use in web applications.

One major problem posited by Turing-complete machines (i.e. any machine capable of running scripts written in a Turing-complete language) is known as the "halting problem." Basically, this means is that the computer has no way of knowing in advance whether a program will stop at some point, or if it will loop forever and ever and ever (in programming terms, this is known as an "infinite loop"). The only way to determine this is by actually running the code.

For example, imagine I had a program that said something like: "Dear computer, please give me a random number." While it is possible that I could get a number like 50 or 300, you might also notice that I did not specify a length. It is entirely possible that the computer would spit out a number so long that, if unchecked, it could go on and on and on towards infinity. A better idea might be to tell the computer, "Dear computer, please give me a random number less than 1000." Then, of course, it could spit out a negative number that headed on towards infinity. So, I might tell it, "Ok, fine, please give me a random number between 0 and 1000." The poor computer is just trying to do its job, but this time it might spit out a number like 1.500000... followed by infinite 0's. Really, to get our program to work, we would need to specify that we want a whole number, or integer, between 0 and 1000.

Getting programs to run the way we want them to is not always easy, and it is not uncommon for programming bugs to lead inadvertently to "infinite loops." A machine has no way of knowing whether or not it will run into an infinite loop in a piece of code until it actually runs that code, at which point it is stuck. If any node on the Ethereum network got stuck running a program in an infinite loop, it would effectively halt the entire system, hence being called "the halting problem." This inability to complete a script would stop new data from being added to the blockchain. That would be bad. So, how can we avoid this problem?

The answer is actually pretty simple: Ether. Within the Ethereum network, computation is not free. Every time a user makes a request to run a script, a certain fee is associated, which is paid in Ether. Furthermore, in order to run a script, a user must set a limit to the amount of Ether put towards running that script. The Ether dedicated to running a particular script is known as "gas." If the script runs out of Ether, or "gas", before completion, it will simply halt at its current state.

By requiring a fee and forcing a value cap to be set for each script, Ethereum eliminates the problem of infinitely looping programs, be they accidental, or, as is more likely the case, malicious denial-of-service attacks. Nobody has an infinite amount of Ether, so even if a bad actor attempted to execute an infinitely looping program, they would not be able to sustain the funding required to continue running the program. The script would be cut off from executing as soon as the funding ran out.

Ether, as a currency, plays an integral role in the Ethereum framework. Outside of usage as "gas" towards executing smart contracts on the Ethereum blockchain, however, Ether is also traded on many popular exchanges for other cryptocurrencies and some fiat currencies, like dollars and euros.

In the US, you can buy Ether with fiat currency through several digital currency exchanges, including Coinbase, Bittrex, and others. You can buy Ether with Bitcoin through almost all notable exchanges, including ShapeShift, Kraken, Poloniex, and more. Depending on where you are in the world, your access to specific exchanges will vary, but you should have no trouble buying, selling, or trading Ether through one or more online platforms no matter where you live.

Ether has a significant real-world value beyond the role of "gas." One Ether has reached a value of over $300 at several periods throughout 2017. For many, Ether is treated exclusively as an investment, with speculators exchanging Bitcoin or other digital currencies for Ether in hopes that the value of Ether will increase. If it does, they may simply trade their Ether back into fiat without ever really engaging with any applications on the Ethereum network. In this sense, Ether can be bought, sold, and traded like Bitcoin or any other digital currency. Within the Ethereum framework, however, Ether serves a unique purpose as "gas" for running smart contracts.

Even if your interest in Ethereum is purely as a financial investment and you don't plan on writing software or being involved in any way with applications built on the platform, it is helpful to understand the relationship between those applications, the structure of the Ethereum ecosystem, and the value of Ether as a currency.

We know that Ether can be bought on various currency exchanges, but where does Ether actually come from? Who makes it and how? As of the time of this writing, Ether is "mined" in a manner similar to Bitcoin. Nodes in the Ethereum network perform complex math problems in order to validate transactions. When a particular node, or miner, successfully "solves a block," that block is added to the blockchain and the miner is rewarded for their work with a certain amount of Ether. This structure may be changing in the near future, however, and this leads us to another important concept.

We need to look a bit more closely at the role of mining, how transactions are validated, how the blockchain is maintained, and how this relates to the future of Ethereum.

Consensus Algorithms:
Proof-of-Work vs. Proof-of-Stake

A significant part of what drives the real-world implementation of blockchain protocols involves conducting secure transactions, whether they are purely financial transactions as with Bitcoin or whether they are transactions of other types of information or data. When one party sends information to another, how does the system guarantee that the information is valid?

We have touched already on the concept of a distributed ledger, and the role of decentralized networks in maintaining a blockchain. As a practical matter, what this means is that many people all over the world need to run software that validates transactions and records those transactions on the blockchain. In some cases, this can get quite expensive in terms of both computer power and electricity. To encourage people to participate, we can imagine that they might need some incentive. This is where "mining" comes in.

Bitcoin miners notoriously require specialized equipment that perform thousands of complex mathematical operations every second. These calculations eat up significant processing power and consume a lot of electricity. We will not go too in depth into how Bitcoin mining works specifically, but the general idea is that miners compete to solve a complex math problem in order to validate each new block that is added to the blockchain.

The solution to the problem, each time, is basically a random number, and the only way to find it is by trial and error. So, miners use their equipment to try out random numbers as quickly as possible until they find one that matches the criteria set forth by the core code of the Bitcoin software. When a miner thinks they have found a solution, they broadcast this to the entire Bitcoin network and other miners check their solution. When a majority of miners agrees that the solution is correct, the block is added to the blockchain and the miner who found the solution is rewarded with a brand new Bitcoin that is generated from the Bitcoin software. For active miners, the potential for earning the reward outweighs the cost incurred by running mining equipment, which encourages participation in the system.

This model is known as the "Proof-of-Work" model because the only way to solve the problem required to validate a block is via trial and error. There is no way for a miner to produce a correct result and get the reward other than by doing the work of computation.

Like Bitcoin, Ethereum has historically worked on a "Proof-of-Work" consensus model. However, in early 2017, it was announced that Ethereum intends to shift towards implementing a "Proof-of-Stake" consensus model in the near future. Vitalik Buterin, Ethereum's creator, released a whitepaper in May of 2017 proposing the implementation of a new Proof-of-Stake algorithm called Casper into the Ethereum protocol. The timeframe remains unclear, but early reports suggest that the Casper algorithm will be phased in over time.

Ethereum enthusiasts have met this news with mixed feelings, and there is ongoing speculation as to how Proof-of-Stake will translate into real-world applications.

In order to understand how this might impact Ethereum, let's explore how Proof-of-Stake generally works. When looking at Proof-of-Work, we saw that there is a real-world cost associated with performing what are essentially meaningless calculations in order to find a random number to solve a block and claim a reward. To get a sense of how significant this cost is, it is estimated that both Bitcoin and Ethereum eat up over $1 million **per day** in electricity and hardware costs associated with mining.

Ethereum's proposed Proof-of-Stake (PoS) model eliminates the resource drain presented by PoW. Rather than relying on miners, participants in this model take on the role of "validators." Similar to placing a bet, validators stake a certain amount of their own Ether towards solving a block. The higher the amount a validator stakes, the greater the probability that they will solve the block. If they "win," they will be rewarded.

In the event that a bad actor attempts to manipulate the system, their stake will simply disappear out of circulation. The Ether they have put towards attempting to validate a false transaction, for example, will be eliminated from the total amount of Ether in existence. In theory, this will increase the overall value of the currency due to the principle of scarcity. In economics, the scarcity principle basically implies that where there is demand, the less of a commodity there is, the greater its value.

ETHEREUM

The Casper algorithm represents a new model for implementing Proof-of-Stake consensus in a real-world environment. Among Ethereum users and throughout the larger cryptocurrency and blockchain community, there is much ongoing debate over PoW versus PoS, both in general and in relation to Ethereum specifically.

If successful, some of the advantages of Proof-of-Stake include the aforementioned elimination of resource consumption required for mining, and potentially a greater level of security and scalability.

Faster transaction speeds may also be a result. However, until the Casper algorithm is implemented, many of these possibilities remain theoretical, and many skeptics maintain the attitude of, "I'll believe it when I see it."

As a platform for handling smart contracts, Ethereum opens up the potential of blockchain technology for a wide variety of applications by creating a secure, hack-proof, trustless environment for creating and executing smart contracts. Fundamental to this platform is the way in which transactions of information are validated, and validation is handled by the consensus algorithm. Consensus algorithms are a big deal in terms of the functionality of a decentralized blockchain environment. Naturally, there are those who are apprehensive and have concerns about how shifting the consensus algorithm from Proof-of-Work to Proof-of-Stake may impact Ethereum. Some, of course, believe that Proof-of-Stake will present a positive evolution in terms of improving the efficiency of the blockchain architecture.

Consensus Algorithms: Proof-of-Work vs. Proof-of-Stake

Will Proof-of-Stake actually perform as intended when implemented in the real world? The answer remains to be seen, but for those with a vested interest in Ethereum, this is an important space to watch moving forward.

Ethereum (ETH) vs. Ethereum Classic (ETC)

For those who are in the early stages of discovering the cryptocurrency space, one hurdle that you may run into is the existence of Ethereum Classic, abbreviated as ETC on many popular exchanges and cryptocurrency tickers. What is the difference between Ethereum and Ethereum Classic?

If you aren't confused enough already, in order to understand Ethereum Classic it is necessary, also, to become familiar with The DAO. DAO, in general, stands for "decentralized autonomous organization." **The DAO** was a specific decentralized autonomous organization that was launched on the Ethereum blockchain in 2016.

The DAO was designed to offer a model for a new kind of institutional structure, useful for both businesses and non-profit organizations. This particular venture issued a token sale in May of 2016 as a way to crowd-fund development. This token sale was very successful and raised around $150-million in under a month. Then, The DAO's code was hacked just one month later, in June of 2016. Hackers used a known vulnerability in the code to reallocate around one-third of the money into a different account, valued at around $50 million at the time of the attack.

ETHEREUM

In July of 2016, after the hack, there was a decision within the Ethereum community to "hard-fork" the blockchain. A "fork" in a blockchain is much a like a fork in a road- a split, where one path becomes two. In the case of Ethereum, hard-forking the blockchain made it possible to go back and recover the stolen funds and return them to The DAO.

The DAO hard-fork created a large dispute within the Ethereum community. A significant number of participants in the network were against splitting the blockchain, and as a result, they continued to maintain the pre-forked chain. The pre-forked version of the blockchain became Ethereum Classic. The other members of the Ethereum network moved over to the new blockchain, which continued on as Ethereum. Since then, Ethereum has forked a few more times in response to other attacks, strengthening its defenses against DDoS attacks and spamming. The subsequent forks were not nearly as controversial and did not spawn "competing versions" of Ethereum.

There continues to be an ongoing debate within the Ethereum community over the role of Ethereum Classic and the larger politics surrounding blockchain forks. There are some who are ideologically opposed to the idea of forking, no matter what, arguing that the inherent value and guiding principle of a blockchain are that it cannot be altered. Others believe that forking can be a necessary, acceptable, and useful way for blockchain projects to adapt in response to changing circumstances, technological advances, and user demands.

Debate exists concerning investment viability as well as ideology. There are those who will assert that Ethereum Classic is "dead," and there are those who believe it will ultimately overtake Ethereum as the dominant "fork" of the blockchain, the latter of which are a minority. Looking at the history of both in terms of their respective currencies, it is safe to say that the majority of investors seem to trend, thus far, towards Ethereum rather than Ethereum Classic.

Mining with Ethereum

Should you be new to Ethereum mining, then you are going to have to go through some steps to make sure that you are using Ethereum correctly.

1. Install C++ visual

The first thing that you must do is download the visual package for C ++ from Microsoft. You are either going to have to choose vcreditst_x64 or vcredist_x86 depending on the system that you are working on. To check and see which system you have, go to the Microsoft page and go to automatic version detection results.

Note: you are going to want to work with a 64 bit system if possible. 32 bit systems are going to experience errors as you are working with mining.

2. Install Ethereum

Now you need to download Mist. Mist is a graphical user interface that is friendly and familiar. It is going to contain a wallet for Ethereum that will be the location where your mining profits are going to go. There is also a browser that will allow you to talk to other miners and even tutorials that are going to show you how to work with Mist.

3. Get blockchain

You will need to download the blockchain and wait as it syncs. The download is over 10 gigs, so you are going to be waiting a while. While this is going on, you may want to get familiar with Mist and the interface so that you are not worried about what is going on in the program when you are working with it.

4. Set your wallet up

The Ethereum wallet is going to need to be opened and a new account started before you can choose your wallet type. Your wallet is going to have a payout address where your rewards will go.

5. Install AMD open CL SDK or Nvidia Cuda

Depending on the GPU you are working with, you need to download AMD or Nvidia.

6. Install AlethOne miner

A simple miner is going to be a GUI download, and the mining software for AlethOne is going to depend on the package you are using in Visual C ++. Keep in mind that a 32-bit system is going to have problems mining.

7. Wait for DAG initialization

Once you have completed your installation, you are going to have to wait for around ten minutes while your miner builds a DAG. The DAG is a 1 GB file that is going to be stored in the RAM of the GPU to make the algorithm memory hard and therefore ASIC resistant.

After your DAG is completed, you can begin solo mining with AlethOne so that you can ensure everything is working as it is supposed to.

8. Join a mining pool

Here you are going to have to set up a mining pool. Solo mining is not going to get you any ether unless you are working with a warehouse full of GPU.

Ethereum Enterprise Alliance

It was in March of 2017 that blockchain startups, Fortune 500 companies, and research groups decided that they were going to create the Enterprise Ethereum Alliance, otherwise known as the EEA.

The Ethereum Enterprise Alliance is a nonprofit organization that works with over a hundred and sixteen different members including companies such as Microsoft, Intel, and the National Bank of Canada.

The EEA was created to coordinate an open source standard that would be a private and permissioned version of Ethereum that would be able to address anything from banking to entertainment and everything that falls in between. Along with that, it is going to address and work with the ecosystem that is Ethereum.

There are members of the Ethereum Enterprise Alliance that have said that they want to work with things such as hybrid architectures so that they can try and anchor to private blockchains and make them open to the public.

The Ethereum blockchain may come to contain things that open just to companies while other things are open to the public. In the end, they are trying to bridge block chains that are permissioned with those that do not have any permissions.

ETHEREUM

There are some projects that are being investigated as permissioned blockchains such as:

1. The Royal Bank of Scotland: there was an announcement that a clearing and settlement mechanism was created based on the distributed ledger that Ethereum works on as well as the smart contract platform.

2. JP Morgan Chase: a block chain is being built onto the Ethereum that has been dubbed quorum and is going to stand right in the line of private and public for payments in Ethereum. This idea was developed so that the regulators could be satisfied as to who needed access to the goings on for the financial department as well as keeping the privacy of those that used their bank.

Programming with Ethereum

The smart contracts in Ethereum are abstracts that operate at a high-level while being compiled on EVM bytecode and then sent over the Ethereum blockchain to be executed. Most smart contracts are written in Solidity, Serpent, LLL, and Mutan.

Each programming language that is used in Ethereum is also in other languages such as JavaScript or Python.

Research has been going on within Ethereum to create a new language known as Viper. This language is supposed to be a Python derived language that is going to work strictly with Ethereum.

Any smart contract that is written in Ethereum is going to be stored publicly on the block chain. The biggest downside to this is that there are going to be performance issues with the nodes in calculating the smart contracts in real time as well as decreased operating speeds.

The engineers working on this are working on sharding the calculations, but so far, no solution has been found. However, in January of 2016, the protocol was made to be able to process 25 transactions a second. It was not until September of the same year that Buterin presented his idea to increase the scalability of the program.

ETHEREUM

This platform has several processes that are being used. It has been described as shared software that is going to be tamperproof.

The Ethereum platform is decentralized and works with decentralized autonomous organizations and smart contacts along with dozens of other functioning applications that it has been built on.

Smart Contracts

These contracts are going to be able to self-verify the conditions that are set forth in the contract by using the data that they are given, as well as self-executing the release of the payment once the contract has been completed. These contacts run on node networks that can control the contract's participants to ensure that the contract will indeed be executed once it is written, thus ensuring the contract creator that their contract will be executed as they intended.

As the smart contract verifies itself, it will continue to record all the data (in real time) and send it to the pre-defined data feeds such as the price, location, etc. While it does that, it will also release the payments to the proper parties once the key conditions have been met.

Smart contracts are tamper-resistant, meaning that because they run on a network of computers that no human can influence, they cannot be changed. The only thing that can be changed is the obligations laid out in the smart contract before it is sent off to this database of computers to be executed. The owner of the smart contract will have the satisfaction of knowing that their contract will be executed as they wrote it out.

The high efficiency of the way that these contracts are valued is a benefit for this type of technology. Large companies such as insurance and trade finance companies will be able to see a large jump in profits due to the low cost of the smart contract.

With the ability to eliminate multiple people checking on the different data sources for the proof of performance as the contract is now able to do this itself, the cost is lowered because there is no need to hire extra workers. This also means the check for the performance is done faster and more efficiently.

You are also able to reference the private system as well as the companies that make smart contracts. Being that they are tamper-proof, you can rely on the trigger of any payment to be done properly and without human error.

An 'oracle' that sits between the external world and a smart contract provides the data that is needed for the contract to prove its performance. It also sends all commands to the external systems where they belong.

When you look at networks such as Ethereum, you will realize that there is an input/output limitation because of the security constraints that are in place that only allow for limited access to anything that is not on the network.

Because of this, things such as the contractual performance and payments are outside of the network. There must be a secured point which connects the smart contract to the outside points that they need access to.

These oracles are known for their ability to get data from any outside source that the system is unable to acquire on its own. These oracles work as both inbound and outbound oracles which do what a smart contract is supposed to do, such as release payments or perform the bylines in the contract.

Inbound oracles can provide smart contracts with external data so that they are able to determine if the events that are happening outside of the smart contract are required.

Outbound oracles allow the contract to be able to access the internal command systems as well as release any payments that should be released.

A private smart contract data storage is the most natural way that oracles use to interact with the external sources that Ethereum is not able to access. Should the data feed allow a rather large result, there are hundreds of values that are created to fully prove contractual performance. At that point in time, the oracle would then be able to provide all the records needed, as well as retain all the detailed data that is preset to be passed by only the most critical of values so that they can prove performance in the smart contract.

Only the most critical information is moved along from the external systems to the smart contract. Because of the elevated level of privacy, there is no way to be able to tell the smart contract code what is relative from an outside network.

If you pre-set the oracle so that only the most critical of information is passed through, then you will have almost eliminated all need for the information about the smart contract's context and purpose, therefore, providing it with more privacy when running on a larger network.

When you are looking at smart contracts, you will see that they are nothing more than a program that is written using the

ETHEREUM

Ethereum level programming language, which uses either Solidity or Serpent depending on how you want to read it on your computer.

The contract is meant to enforce a deal between two or more parties to get a specific product out of one or more of the interested parties. For example, if there is something that you want to sell, however, your interested buyer is not able to pay until a later date, you can then make a smart contract that will enable them to send Ether to your Ether wallet on that specific date. Once the obligations of the contract have been fulfilled, he then gets what he has paid for. This is called an interest of things.

Ultimately, in the future, these contracts are all going to be enforced unambiguously by a system of computers that will not release any payments until all obligations to any contractual agreements have been fulfilled. Should the agreements not be fulfilled specifically to the owner's specifications, no payment will be released.

The smart contracts are stored on a blockchain which is protected by the Ethereum system, which is ultimately nothing more than a system of networked computers that has been decentralized, ensuring that every transaction can be verified by using a peer to peer network. There are no third parties involved when it comes to a smart contract.

Unlike a normal contract that is written up by a person, the words in a smart contract are clear and concise so that both parties understand what is being asked of them and what is expected of them. Ethereum has given the programming language that they use the whole purpose of making sure that it is an unambiguous language so it is very clear who is right and who is wrong regarding the contract.

This prevents evens where two people within a contract must go to trial and figure out who is wrong and who is right. Both parties of the contract are held to their respective ends of the contract before anything can be completed.

As the owner of the contract, you are held to the obligation of paying out the respective amount of Ether that you have promised for the work that you are receiving. If you are not completely happy with the work that you have gotten back, you are not obligated to pay out the fee until you get the work that you have specifically requested from the other party.

As the other party, you are expected to do exactly the work that the owner of the contract is expecting to receive. Just as you would want the best work that someone could give you, you're obligated to give him or her the absolute best work that you can. Once you have completed it to their specifications, you will then be able to receive the compensation that you were promised when you first signed the contract.

Both parties are protected from not getting the work that they have requested and not getting the payment that they have been promised. If at any point in time, one who is fulfilling the requests of the contract does not know what it is they are to do, they are able to look back at their contract and see; because as we've stated, the language in the smart contracts is created to be very plain in order for everyone involved to understand.

Should you want to make your own smart contract, there are a few steps that you need to go through to make this happen.

First, you're going to need to download a program called Solidity. This is a program that is very like JavaScript, but uses a different coding language. However, if this doesn't interest you, then you can always use a web-based coder such as Cosmo. Whichever one you choose, it is going to be the program that you'll use when writing the code for your smart contract.

If you go the way of Cosmo, you have the added benefit of being able to simply send your contract straight to the network once you have compiled it the way that you want it to be. Once it is there, you will access it using a program called Ethereum Web3.ja. However, it is important that even if you are using Cosmo you must follow the steps below to make sure that your contract is uploaded to the nodes correctly. If you do not follow all the steps, then you are endangering yourself. Your contract may not respond fast enough or may fail the tests that are required to be run on it. You may even run into the possibility that your contract does not get put onto the blockchain for Ethereum.

Once your contract is on the network, it will be distributed to the appropriate application framework. In doing this, it will make it easier for you as you won't have to upload everything about the contract. This also helps lower human error. But, you are still going to be required to do some work. The framework is just going to be there to help guide you through the following steps and help keep you from making errors. Nothing is going to be a hundred percent error free because a human has touched everything that has been created, therefore, you may very well make a mistake. Thankfully, before your contract is live on Ethereum, you are going to be able to go back and have an interaction with your contract to make sure everything is correct.

Some of the frameworks that are available for you to use are Truffle, Embark, and Meteor, as well as API.

Okay, now that we've gone over the programming that you're going to need to make your smart contract, let's go over the actual steps that you're going to use to make these contracts. Please remember that each contract is going to be different based on the person who is writing it. Not only that, but every person is going to make their contract differently.

These steps can be found in more detail in the book, *Blockchain: The Ultimate Guide to Understanding the Hidden Economy* by Osar Flynt.

1. You're going to need to create what is known as an Ethereum node. To do this, you're going to need a program called Geth, which allows accessibility of the main interface that is used when an Ethereum node is implemented. (To get Geth, you will be able to go to www.Ethereum.org). Any other programs that you could possibly need are either on the Ethereum website, or the website will have a link for you to be able to go to a trusted site and get them. Be careful of where you are downloading programs: some of the programs that you need could end up having a virus in them that will get into your computer and cause you issues later. Only download from trusted sites.

2. Once you have downloaded the appropriate program and have launched it correctly, you're then going to compile the smart contract that you have created using the Solidity program we talked about earlier or the Cosmo program we also talked about. Both programs are going to go over your contract and make sure that everything is correct for you, however, it will not approve it without your permission just in case you decide that there is something else that you want to add to your contract at a later point in time.

3. When you have deployed your smart contract, you will be spending ether to have your contract on the server. You will also be required to sign the contract stating that it is your contract and everything that you have compiled into it is correct.

4. Once you've done this, you will then receive a blockchain address and ABI to your contract. Now, should you need to, you are able to call your contract back by using your API and changing it as needed. Just be careful, because you could end up spending more ether with every interaction that you have with your contract.

Now that you've created your smart contract and put it out on the Ethereum platform, you're going to want to test your work just like with anything else that you create. The purpose of testing your contract is to make sure that it meets all the requirements that Ethereum requires of their contracts. While you are the sole owner of the contract and are the one who determines what work you want to be done, there are still certain aspects that Ethereum needs to look at and make sure they are correct. To do this, there are just a few simple steps that you can follow.

Once again, you can find more detailed steps to testing your work in *Blockchain: The Ultimate Guide to Understanding the Hidden Economy.*

When you're testing your transaction times, you're going to want to try and make sure that it takes a minimum of ten seconds for any transaction to be verified. This is because of the decentralized applications that Ethereum uses to self-verify the applications and contracts that are on their system. Before you do this, it probably best that you use a basic smart contract to see how it works before using your own contract. Not only will this allow you to go through the process and get the hang of it, but it will also keep you from potentially messing up and losing your contract, or worse, changing the terms of your contract that you did not want to change.

1. You're going to want to have a program installed that will access your Ethereum nodes, such as Solidity. It is also important that you keep your python library completely separate from the virtual environment that you are currently using. In doing this, you are making sure that you are not crossing anything in the library with what you have written, nor are you placing your contract in the wrong place by mistake.

2. Now you're going to want to start a new client node while using the console window. After starting Truffle in your resulting window, you're then going to type in a command such as "truffle deploy" so that you will be able to create what is known as a boilerplate contract.

On top of that, the program will begin to automatically search for any errors you may come across as you're testing your transaction times. It is important to remember that your target time for transactions is about ten seconds. Anything more than that is too long, and you may have trouble finding someone to take your contract.

3. As you are developing your contract, it is beneficial to run a compile in the Truffle program so that you can ensure that your contract will comply properly.

You also have the option to test deploy onto the Ethereum networks and run a test there if you wish to.

At this point, you have created your contract and tested it. Now it is time to put your contract out on the network! To deploy your contract, you're still going to be using the Truffle program.

1. To begin, you're going to type in the command "truffle init" so that you can create a new directory.

2. Once you're done that, you're going to find your contract in the directory.

3. Then go to config/app.json and add your contract into the contracts space that is provided by Truffle.

4. Now you'll need to restart your node (in a separate window) so that you can run the command "tesrpc".

5. At this point, you are now ready to run your root directory and make sure that you contract is on the network as you want it.

It is good idea to write a test for your new code to make sure that it works properly. You're going to want to go to the folder that is relative to the test directory and rename your file so that you can distinguish the two.

Once you're done that, run your test using Truffle and your root directory. The goal is to make sure that the test passes.

Now that the test has been run, add all UI to your Truffle Directory. Once you've done this, you're once again going to have to run Truffle so that the UI will automatically be compiled and configured into your contract so that it can be created in the directory that you want it to be in.

You may want to recompile your contract regularly to make sure that the application is running properly and any changes that you've made are reflected in the Truffle program.

The App Directory will already have some boiler points in it that are going to help with the UI and distribution of your contract. If you want to access it, then you are going to want to start the Truffle Watch process before reopening your root directory in a browser window.

At this point in time, you'll want to open the developer and then right click to choose which option it is you want to inspect. While you're on this screen, you should add in the "window. onload" function so that you can ensure your contract is activated once your page loads.

Copy all your functions to make sure that you can remove all the testing assertions before as well as making sure that your output is returned to normal and working properly with the console.

As a result, you should have the starting balance, the balance that the changes predetermined, and any changes that have officially occurred, as well as if a refund has been requested.

From here, all you'll need to do is load Meteor and work on your UI so that you can use it to interact with the contract that you have created therefore ensuring that any interactions you make are as simple and painless as possible.

Making the Use of Ethereum Easier

I n this chapter, you are going to learn a few tips and tricks that are going to make the use of Ethereum easier. These small tricks will normally be created by other users who are going to discover a solution for a problem that they experienced.

The tips and tricks that you use with Ethereum, you are going to be able to use with Bitcoin as they are similar programs with similar program styles. However, you have to be careful because some of the tips and tricks are going to be more effective on one platform over the other.

1. Keep separate wallets: just like with your money, it is not wise to keep a lot of money in one place, so why would you do it with your digital money? You should keep the spending apart from the ether that you are trying to save. If you have it in multiple places then you are going to be lowering the risk of spending all of the ether that you have in your possession. You are also going to be lowering the risk of people who are going to want to hack your account to get what you have. Thankfully, you are not limited to the number of wallets that you can have. So, it is best that you have a wallet for spending and a wallet for receiving.

2. Don't keep your savings in a web wallet: a web wallet can be hacked! Due to this, you are going to end up

losing all of your ether savings if you are not careful. Web wallets are convenient, however, they should only be used like a checking account; a place to store your money that is not going to be sitting there for an extended period of time. So, if you end up being hacked, you will only lose a small amount of money rather than everything that is in your possession. You should remember that ether is not going to work like a credit card, if you lose money, no matter how much, you are not going to get it back since there is no way that you can claim that it was lost. While you are going to be able to go to the police, they are not likely to do anything because there is no way of knowing who got ahold of the money that was taken.

3. Protect your privacy: you would not give someone your pin number, you should not give anyone the information to get into your online wallet either. While it is possible that someone can figure out which wallets are yours thanks to transaction history, it is not likely that they are going to get both of your wallets. There is no better way to keep your wallet private than keeping your pin to yourself. Whenever you are transferring money you should use a service that is going to scramble the signal so that you can make it harder for someone to find all of your wallets.

4. Cold storage: your wallet information should not be kept on your computer due to the fact that someone can hack into your computer and get your account information. However, it really does not matter because they can hack your account if they really want to. The wallets that are used for Ethereum and Bitcoin are best

known for keeping their data in locations that are predictable as well as vulnerable to attacks from things like Trojan horses. It is best that you keep the private key for your wallet offline so that you can offer yourself a little bit of extra protection. Your offline solutions could be QR codes that you print off onto a piece of paper or a plain text file that is going to be stored on a USB. If you want to transfer your coins to an offline wallet, you are going to need to have the QR code and the private key to the wallet. You will then be able to see the balance of your wallet. If you are still not happy with this level of protection, then you can encrypt your key so that no one but yourself can get into your wallet.

5. Backup: though it won't matter if you work with blockchain platforms, you are going to need to back up the work that you complete. This will protect you and all of your earnings from others. When you use the backup feature, your public and private keys will be saved in a file that you can retrieve when you want to. The value of your wallet is tied to the address where your wallet's data will be stored. This is not going to be your actual wallet application. However, when you have a file that contains your wallet and any other information you need to access it, it will be stored in a safe location of your choosing.

To end this chapter, I am going to reiterate that it is vital that you keep your login information private. If you do not, then you are allowing someone into your account and it is going to be like giving someone your information to get into your bank account, which of course you wouldn't do. In the end, they are the same thing. Digital currency and regular currency can both be stolen, so protect yourself so that you do not get robbed!

A hacker is going to do anything that they possibly can to gain access to your account, so if you are not careful, you are going to get your virtual wallet hacked. But, unlike with your real money, you are not going to be able to get it back and you will just have to accept the loss.

Ethereum's Enterprise Alliance

March 2017 was when the fortune 500 companies, blockchain startups, and several research groups got together and decided that they would create the EEA, the Ethereum Enterprise Alliance.

This alliance is a nonprofit organization that works with over a hundred and sixteen members such as Microsoft, the National Bank of Canada, Intel, and so many more.

The Ethereum Enterprise Alliance was first created in order to coordinate an open source standard that is a private as well as a permissioned version of Ethereum that can address a wide variety of topics from banking to entertainment and everything in between. On top of that, it also addresses a work and ecosystem that is built inside of Ethereum that these companies are going to work off of so that they can not only work together, but also so they can achieve the goals that they set for themselves.

Some of the members of the Ethereum Enterprise Alliance have reported that they are going to start new projects, such as hybrid architecture, in order to allow them to anchor a private block chain so that they can turn it around and make it public and everyone can get onto it. This opens up a lot of possibilities not only for the company, but for other people as well. Possibilities that they may never have gotten before had not been for that particular company.

ETHEREUM

Ethereum's blockchain is constantly evolving and it may even come to contain aspects that will be open to just large companies, while there are other aspects that are open to the entire public. What it all comes down to is that the companies working on Ethereum are attempting to bridge block chains that are permissioned to the ones that do not have any permissions.

Some projects that are trying to use permissioned block chains are being investigated and here are a few of those projects that are under investigation.

1. Scotland's Royal Bank has made an announcement that it is creating a clearing and settlement tool that will create a distribution ledger that Ethereum is going to work with based off of the smart contract platform which is open for users to write smart contracts on.

2. A block chain has been built on Ethereum by JP Morgan Chase and has been dubbed quorum. This makes it possible for it to stand right on the line between public and private when it comes to payments being received or sent out on Ethereum's platform. This idea came from the regulators who required access to everything that was occurring in the financial department and needing to protect the privacy of those who use their bank so that they do not lose their business.

The Virtual Machine of Ethereum

Ethereum's virtual machine will focus on the security and execution of the code that is untrusted but is computed by computers to be used all over the world. Should you want to break it down even more, you will be focusing on the DOS attacks and how you can prevent them or the denial of service attacks that are becoming more and more prevalent in the world of cryptocurrency. Not just that, but the virtual machine will ensure that other programs cannot access the state of a different program by ensuring communication can be established without interference.

Ethereum uses a virtual machine that will run as a run time environment for the smart contracts located in Ethereum. There are a lot of people who use cryptocurrency who have been made aware of what smart contracts are and how popular they are quickly becoming. This technology can be used to conduct transactions through an automated system or perform tasks that are on the block chain without supervision. Some believe that smart contracts are going to eventually revolutionize the financial industry in the years to come.

It is known that the virtual machine has been mentioned in a paper that Dr. Gavin Wood wrote, which was leading people to think that Ethereum was constructed to introduce a sandboxed environment that will change the entire future. There is one piece of code that will help to make Ethereum better than other platforms and that is that smart contracts are being used.

When it comes to sandboxed environments, you will not be able to see the full potential that it holds for technology due to the fact that it is in its initial states and constantly changing.

Whenever looking at the day to day operations that can be decentralized, you will realize that it is the virtual machine in charge of making sure these tasks are completed.

Not just that, but the virtual machine is valuable, and most importantly it is free! What programmer would pass up on that?

The Ecosystem of Ethereum

Clients and wallets of Ethereum

- Parity: implementation in Rust

- Cpp- Ethereum: an implementation of C ++

- MyEtherWallet: a wallet that is found online

- Gerth: a Go implementation

- Mist: a desktop wallet

- Hyperledger Burrow: the virtual machine's implementation in Go that was made by Monax

- Ledger nano S: a hardware wallet for your ether

- Jaxx: a web wallet

- KeepKey: another hardware wallet

Decentralized applications

- Digital signatures will ensure that there is a proof of existence for the documents that are used by the Luxembourg Stock Exchange.

- There are identity systems in place to make sure that they are secure for the internet through a port known as uPort.

- Some of the interactive grids work for the IoT which will in turn use the assets like bluetooth and other near field communication chips.

- Slock is a program that was developed with smart locks for this reason alone.

- Digital tokens are pegged to fiat currencies through a decentralized capital. The Spanish bank of Santander is responsible for making this happen.

- Digital tokens that are pegged to gold was an idea that came from Digix.

- Some improvements have come along in the way of digital rights for music, too, which works with the piracy laws as well to try and protect artists and make sure that they are getting the money that they are due.

Milestones that Ethereum Has Hit

Ethereum's foundation has developed several different prototypes for the platform as part of a proof of concept series even before the frontier network was launched. One of the last prototypes was released to the public for beta testing under the name Olympic. The network made it so that users could work with a big bounty of 25,000 ether so that the block chain could be tested to see how far it could be stressed by its users.

Once Olympic was released and tested by the Ethereum community, Ethereum announced that the frontier network would move into a new experimental release portion which was set out in the year 2015. Since the launch, Ethereum has advanced and evolved multiple times through several different upgrades that people know as milestones. These changes are vital to the network and are going to affect how the program will work so that the developmental team can make the Ethereum platform more user friendly.

One of the most current milestones that Ethereum has reached was Homestead and it is now considered stable. This milestone was released to help improve the transaction process, gas pricing of Ethereum, and the security that is offered by Ethereum. There are at least two more upgrades that are planned for Ethereum in the future.

ETHEREUM

The first upgrade that is planned is called Metropolis and it is supposed to reduce the complexity of the virtual machine while adding flexibility for everyone who writes smart contracts. But, the other upgrade, which was dubbed Serenity is not nearly as clear cut on what it is supposed to be changing on the Ethereum platform. It is rumored that it will change the consensus algorithm which is currently being used by Ethereum. Therefore, there is a basic transition that is going to come from the hardwiring of mining and the virtual mining that takes place in Ethereum.

These improvements will also work on sharding. 2016 brought the DAO which is a decentralized autonomous organization which sets contracts that are meant to assist in developing the platform. The platform is based on raising up to a hundred and fifty million dollars, if not more, through crowdfunding to fund the project. The DAO ended up exploiting fifty million dollars in ether to an anonymous entity.

Because of this event, there was a debate in the crypto community in regards to performing a hard fork so that it can return funds that have been stolen. Due to the dispute being so big, the community started to split into two different groups. One group was those who rejected the update and wanted to use Ethereum classic which was Ethereum before the fork update occurred. And the other group contained those who accepted the upgrade.

The fork update caused a rivalry between the two networks. One side decided that they wanted to work with the classic version and desired the block chain to be immutable while the other side wanted an eternity and a decentralized decision making process.

Of course there are people who are going to criticize the people who use the classic version by saying that the classic version is nothing but a scam and is stealing intellectual property from the developers of the program, however, these remarks are being made by the other side as well.

Ethereum classic still has users that have used Ethereum, but it has also brought in those who use other forms of cryptocurrency, those who did not like the fork ideology. This project is not supported by Ethereum officially, therefore, it is not going to be endorsed by the developers, miners, business partners, or anyone else of Ethereum.

After all the hard fork disputes, Ethereum forked two times in their fourth quarter of 2016 in order to deal with other attacks that came about. In November of 2016, Ethereum had to increase their DOS protection, thwart those who would wish to spam attack in the future, and even de-bloat their block chain.

Conclusion

Congratulations!

You made it to the end of the book and I hope it offered you all of the information that you were wishing to find out about Ethereum.

Ethereum is a wonderful mining platform that continues to develop as it moves along. It is important that you keep in mind that Ethereum is still very young and in its developmental stages, but that is not holding it back from making the most out of the platform that it is offering its users.

You may discover that you want to use Ethereum and Bitcoin together and that is perfectly fine. If you are switching over from Bitcoin, you are going to have a little bit of an understanding of Ethereum as it comes from the same family, however, it is not going to be exactly the same due to the fact that the developers took a different route in regards to actually building the platform for Ethereum.

Learning Ethereum is going to be a process and it is important that you are patient with it and know that you are going to make mistakes and that it is okay. You will be able to learn as you go!

ETHEREUM

If you found this book useful, please leave a review on the website in which you purchased it so that I know how helpful it was to you.

Thank you and good luck on your mining!

About The Book

H ave you ever heard of Bitcoin? Well, Ethereum is very similar and is a platform where you can mine coins known as ether.

Ethereum is a new platform that is continuing to develop and all of the users of Ethereum are going to be a part of history as it continues to grow.

Ethereum will allow you to mine much like Bitcoin, however, the sad thing is that it is still a digital currency that is not accepted everywhere. Although, when it is accepted, you will already have the digital currency built up and will not have to worry about jumping on the bandwagon because you were already on it!